Walker

by

GW00703357

Lang**Syne**
PUBLISHING
WRITING *to* REMEMBER

Lang**Syne**

PUBLISHING

WRITING *to* REMEMBER

79 Main Street, Newtongrange,
Midlothian EH22 4NA
Tel: 0131 344 0414   Fax: 0845 075 6085
E-mail: info@lang-syne.co.uk
www.langsyneshop.co.uk

Design by Dorothy Meikle
Printed by Printwell Ltd
© Lang Syne Publishers Ltd 2019

ISBN 978-1-85217-601-3

Walker

MOTTO:

How great are honourable deeds.

CREST:

An arm in armour with
the hand clutching a lizard.

NAME variations include:
Waulker
Walkere

Chapter one:

The origins of popular surnames

by George Forbes and Iain Gray

***If you don't know where you came from, you won't
know where you're going*** **is a frequently quoted
observation and one that has a particular resonance
today when there has been a marked upsurge in
interest in genealogy, with increasing numbers of
people curious to trace their family roots.**

Main sources for genealogical research
include census returns and official records of births,
marriages and deaths – and the key to unlocking the
detail they contain is obviously a family surname, one
that has been 'inherited' and passed from generation
to generation.

No matter our station in life, we all have a
surname – but it was not until about the middle of the
fourteenth century that the practice of being identified
by a particular surname became commonly established
throughout the British Isles.

Previous to this, it was normal for a person to be identified through the use of only a forename.

But as population gradually increased and there were many more people with the same forename, surnames were adopted to distinguish one person, or community, from another.

Many common English surnames are patronymic in origin, meaning they stem from the forename of one's father – with 'Johnson,' for example, indicating 'son of John.'

It was the Normans, in the wake of their eleventh century conquest of Anglo-Saxon England, a pivotal moment in the nation's history, who first brought surnames into usage – although it was a gradual process.

For the Normans, these were names initially based on the title of their estates, local villages and chateaux in France to distinguish and identify these landholdings.

Such grand descriptions also helped enhance the prestige of these warlords and generally glorify their lofty positions high above the humble serfs slaving away below in the pecking order who had only single names, often with Biblical connotations as in Pierre and Jacques.

The only descriptive distinctions among the peasantry concerned their occupations, like 'Pierre the swineherd' or 'Jacques the ferryman.'

Roots of surnames that came into usage in England not only included Norman-French, but also Old French, Old Norse, Old English, Middle English, German, Latin, Greek, Hebrew and the Gaelic languages of the Celts.

The Normans themselves were originally Vikings, or 'Northmen', who raided, colonised and eventually settled down around the French coastline.

The had sailed up the Seine in their longboats in 900AD under their ferocious leader Rollo and ruled the roost in north eastern France before sailing over to conquer England in 1066 under Duke William of Normandy – better known to posterity as William the Conqueror, or King William I of England.

Granted lands in the newly-conquered England, some of their descendants later acquired territories in Wales, Scotland and Ireland – taking not only their own surnames, but also the practice of adopting a surname, with them.

But it was in England where Norman rule and custom first impacted, particularly in relation to the adoption of surnames.

This is reflected in the famous *Domesday Book*, a massive survey of much of England and Wales, ordered by William I, to determine who owned what, what it was worth and therefore how much they were liable to pay in taxes to the voracious Royal Exchequer.

Completed in 1086 and now held in the National Archives in Kew, London, 'Domesday' was an Old English word meaning 'Day of Judgement.'

This was because, in the words of one contemporary chronicler, "its decisions, like those of the Last Judgement, are unalterable."

It had been a requirement of all those English landholders – from the richest to the poorest – that they identify themselves for the purposes of the survey and for future reference by means of a surname.

This is why the *Domesday Book*, although written in Latin as was the practice for several centuries with both civic and ecclesiastical records, is an invaluable source for the early appearance of a wide range of English surnames.

Several of these names were coined in connection with occupations.

These include Baker and Smith, while Cooks, Chamberlains, Constables and Porters were to be found carrying out duties in large medieval households.

The church's influence can be found in names such as Bishop, Friar and Monk while the popular name of Bennett derives from the late fifth to mid-sixth century Saint Benedict, founder of the Benedictine order of monks.

The early medical profession is represented by Barber, while businessmen produced names that include Merchant and Sellers.

Down at the village watermill, the names that cropped up included Millar/Miller, Walker and Fuller, while other self-explanatory trades included Cooper, Tailor, Mason and Wright.

Even the scenery was utilised as in Moor, Hill, Wood and Forrest – while the hunt and the chase supplied names that include Hunter, Falconer, Fowler and Fox.

Colours are also a source of popular surnames, as in Black, Brown, Gray/Grey, Green and White, and would have denoted the colour of the clothing the person habitually wore or, apart from the obvious exception of 'Green', one's hair colouring or even complexion.

The surname Red developed into Reid, while

Blue was rare and no-one wanted to be associated with yellow.

Rather self-important individuals took surnames that include Goodman and Wiseman, while physical attributes crept into surnames such as Small and Little.

Many families proudly boast the heraldic device known as a Coat of Arms, as featured on our front cover.

The central motif of the Coat of Arms would originally have been what was borne on the shield of a warrior to distinguish himself from others on the battlefield.

Not featured on the Coat of Arms, but high-lighted on page three, is the family motto and related crest – with the latter frequently different from the central motif.

Adding further variety to the rich cultural heritage that is represented by surnames is the appearance in recent times in lists of the 100 most common names found in England of ones that include Khan, Patel and Singh – names that have proud roots in the vast sub-continent of India.

Echoes of a far distant past can still be found in our surnames and they can be borne with pride in commemoration of our forebears.

Chapter two:

Invasion and conquest

Ranked 12th in some lists of the 100 most common surnames found in England today, 'Walker' is an occupational name that has been present from the earliest times.

Derived from the Old English 'wealcare', indicating 'fuller', it denoted someone engaged in the occupation of 'fulling' – the treating and thickening of raw cloth by painstakingly beating it and then trampling, or 'walking' on it as it soaked in water.

Yet another possible derivation is from someone – also known as a fuller – whose duty was to inspect forests, the majority of which in early centuries were owned by the Crown, by 'walking' through them.

Although, in common with many other names found today, 'Walker' was not popularised as a surname until after the Norman Conquest of 1066, those who practised the occupation of fulling were present from a much earlier date.

This means that flowing through the veins of many bearers of the name today may well be the blood of those Germanic tribes who invaded and settled in the south and east of the island of Britain from about the early fifth century.

Known as the Anglo-Saxons, they were composed of the Jutes, from the area of the Jutland Peninsula in modern Denmark, the Saxons from Lower Saxony, in modern Germany and the Angles from the Angeln area of Germany.

It was the Angles who gave the name 'Engla land', or 'Aengla land' – better known as 'England.'

They held sway in what became England from approximately 550 until the Norman Conquest of 1066, with the main kingdoms those of Sussex, Wessex, Northumbria, Mercia, Kent, East Anglia and Essex.

Whoever controlled the most powerful of these kingdoms was tacitly recognised as overall 'king' – one of the most noted being Alfred the Great, King of Wessex from 871 to 899.

It was during his reign that the famous *Anglo-Saxon Chronicle* was compiled – an invaluable source of Anglo-Saxon history – while Alfred was designated in early documents as *Rex Anglorum Saxonum*, King of the English Saxons.

Through the Anglo-Saxons, the language

known as Old English developed, later transforming from the eleventh century into Middle English – sources from which many popular English surnames of today, such as Walker, derive.

The Anglo-Saxons meanwhile, had usurped the power of the indigenous Britons – who referred to them as 'Saeson' or 'Saxones.'

It is from this that the Scottish Gaelic term for 'English people' of 'Sasannach' derives, the Irish Gaelic 'Sasanach' and the Welsh 'Saeson.'

We learn from the *Anglo-Saxon Chronicle* how the religion of the early Anglo-Saxons was one that pre-dated the establishment of Christianity in the British Isles.

Known as a form of Germanic paganism, with roots in Old Norse religion, it shared much in common with the Druidic 'nature-worshipping' religion of the indigenous Britons.

It was in the closing years of the sixth century that Christianity began to take a hold in Britain, while by approximately 690 it had become the 'established' religion of Anglo-Saxon England.

The first serious shock to Anglo-Saxon control came in 789 in the form of sinister black-sailed Viking ships that appeared over the horizon off the island monastery of Lindisfarne, in the northeast of the country.

Lindisfarne was sacked in an orgy of violence and plunder, setting the scene for what would be many more terrifying raids on the coastline of not only England, but also Ireland and Scotland.

But the Vikings, or 'Northmen', in common with the Anglo-Saxons of earlier times, were raiders who eventually stayed – establishing, for example, what became Jorvik, or York, and the trading port of Dublin, in Ireland.

Through intermarriage, the bloodlines of the Anglo-Saxons also became infused with that of the Vikings.

But there would be another infusion of the blood of the 'Northmen' in the wake of the Norman Conquest – a key event in English history that sounded the death knell of Anglo-Saxon supremacy.

By 1066, England had become a nation with several powerful competitors to the throne.

In what were extremely complex family, political and military machinations, the monarch was Harold II, who had succeeded to the throne following the death of Edward the Confessor.

But his right to the throne was contested by

two powerful competitors – his brother-in-law King Harold Hardrada of Norway, in alliance with Tostig, Harold II's brother, and Duke William II of Normandy.

In what has become known as The Year of Three Battles, Hardrada invaded England and gained victory over the English king on September 20 at the battle of Fulford, in Yorkshire.

Five days later, however, Harold II decisively defeated his brother-in-law and brother at the battle of Stamford Bridge.

But he had little time to celebrate his victory, having to immediately march south from Yorkshire to encounter a mighty invasion force, led by Duke William, that had landed at Hastings, in East Sussex.

Harold's battle-hardened but exhausted force confronted the Normans on October 14, drawing up a strong defensive position, at the top of Senlac Hill, building a shield wall to repel Duke William's cavalry and infantry.

The Normans suffered heavy losses, but through a combination of the deadly skill of their archers and the ferocious determination of their cavalry they eventually won the day.

Anglo-Saxon morale had collapsed on the battlefield as word spread through the ranks that

Harold had been killed, and amidst the carnage of the battlefield, it was difficult to identify him – the last of the Anglo-Saxon kings.

William was declared King of England on December 25, and the complete subjugation of his Anglo-Saxon subjects followed.

Within an astonishingly short space of time, Norman manners, customs and law were imposed on England – laying the basis for what subsequently became established 'English' custom and practice.

But beneath the surface, old Anglo-Saxon culture was not totally eradicated, with some aspects absorbed into those of the Normans, while faint echoes of the Anglo-Saxon past is still seen today in the form of popular surnames such as Walker.

Although by its very nature the occupation of fulling, from which 'Walker' derives, was practised throughout the length and breadth of the British Isles, its bearers came to be particularly associated with Yorkshire.

But those of the name who figure prominently in the historical record were not solely confined to this geographical area.

Imprisoned for a time for his strong Puritan views, George Walker was the prominent English clergyman born in 1581 at Hawkshead, in Furness, Lancashire.

Educated at St John's College, Cambridge, he was confirmed as a Church of England minister in April of 1614 and appointed to the rectory of St John Evangelist in the London parish of Watling Street.

Known for his outspoken views on aspects of Church authority and ceremony, he was among those derogatorily referred to at the time as 'Puritans.'

Adopting plain clothing and in favour of more austere forms of worship, these Puritans, who included in their ranks Presbyterians and Calvinists, incurred the wrath of the Church authorities – in particular that of William Laud, who was appointed Archbishop of Canterbury in 1633, during the reign of the ill-fated Stuart monarch Charles I.

During Laud's tenure as Archbishop of Canterbury, the term 'Puritan' became a 'catch-all' term for anyone opposed to his views and his determination to impose uniformity on the Church.

Towards this end, he set up the feared Star Chamber and the High Commission, both of which meted out severe penalties to his detractors.

The clergyman Henry Burton and the lawyer

William Prynne, for example, suffered the penalty of having their ears savagely slashed off.

In November of 1638, George Walker was thrown into prison after a sermon he had preached was deemed to have contained "things tending to faction and disobedient to authority."

But his imprisonment was declared illegal by Parliament in 1641, as the Civil War was about to erupt, and he was released and later restored to his parish.

Charles I had incurred the wrath of Parliament by his insistence on the 'divine right' of monarchs, and added to this was Parliament's fear of Catholic 'subversion' against the state and the king's stubborn refusal to grant demands for religious and constitutional concessions.

Matters came to a head with the outbreak of the Civil War in 1642, with Parliamentary forces, known as the New Model Army and commanded by Oliver Cromwell and Sir Thomas Fairfax, arrayed against the Royalist army of the king.

In what became an increasingly bloody and complex conflict, spreading to Scotland and Ireland and with rapidly shifting loyalties on both sides, the king was eventually captured and executed in January of 1649 on the orders of Parliament.

In 1643, meanwhile, Laud had been impeached by Parliament and executed – one of the charges against him having been the imprisonment of George Walker, who died in 1651.

Also during the Civil War, Robert Walker, born in 1597 in Thorncombe, Devon was the politician and merchant ousted from Parliament in 1643 for his staunch support of the Royalist cause.

Elected Member of Parliament (MP) for Exeter following the Restoration of Charles II in 1660, he held the seat until his death in 1673.

In later centuries, bearers of the Walker name entered the historical record through their contributions to a rich variety of decidedly less turbulent pursuits and endeavours.

Chapter three:

Scientists and entrepreneurs

One particularly inventive bearer of the name and someone whose legacy survives to this day in the form of that indispensable device the friction match was the English chemist John Walker.

Born in 1781 in Stockton-on-Tees, he was first apprenticed as an assistant to the town's surgeon but, finding himself averse to surgery, he turned his attention to chemistry and, after studying the science, he opened a small chemist and druggist business in the town in 1818.

Interested in finding a means to easily create a flame, it was while experimenting with various chemical mixtures known to be capable of ignition by a sudden explosion that a sliver of wood that had been dipped in the mixture took fire after accidently being scraped along his hearth.

Exploiting his discovery, Walker created the first friction matches – wooden splints or sticks of cardboard coated with sulphur and tipped with a mixture of gum, chlorate of potash and sulphide of antimony.

Selling a box of 50 of his matches for one shilling, he also included in the box a piece of sandpaper through which the matches were drawn to ignite them.

Walker named his matches "Congreves", in honour of the rocket pioneer Sir William Congreve.

A modest man, he refused to patent his invention, despite being urged to do so by, for example, the great English scientist Michael Faraday, and it was only after his death in 1859 that he was fully credited as the inventor of the friction match.

In contemporary times, Professor John Walker is the chemist who, along with the American chemist Paul D. Boyer and the Danish Jens C. Skou, shared the Nobel Prize for chemistry in 1997 for work relating to molecular biology, which enhanced the study of genetics.

Born in 1941 in Halifax in the early Walker heartland of Yorkshire and knighted in 1999 for services to molecular biology, he has served as group leader of the mitochondrial biology unit at Cambridge University.

Arthur Walker, born in 1909 in Watford, Hertfordshire, was the British mathematician who, before his death at the age of 90, made pioneering contributions to the fields of physics and physical geometry, while Sir Gilbert Walker was a leading physicist and statistician.

Born in 1868 in Rochdale, Lancashire, he is best remembered for his analysis of the major phenomenon of global climate known as the Southern Oscillation; president from 1926 to 1927 of the Royal Meteorological Society, he died in 1958.

Born in 1805 in Wilmington, Massachusetts, Sears Cook Walker was the American astronomer who investigated the orbit of Neptune and who worked for a time with the United States Naval Observatory; a member of the American Philosophical Society, he died in 1853.

Renowned for his work on photosynthesis, David Walker was the British scientist born in Hull in 1928.

Professor of photosynthesis at the department of animal and plant sciences at Sheffield University, a recipient of the International Society of Photosynthesis Research Communications Award and a Fellow of the scientific think-tank the Royal Society, he died in

2012, having made a significant contribution to the study of plant life.

Bearers of the Walker name have also excelled as entrepreneurs.

Born in 1805 near Kilmarnock, Ayrshire, John Walker, better known as Johnnie Walker, was the founder of what became the internationally famous Scotch whisky brand *Johnnie Walker*.

Left a sum of money in trust following the death of his father in 1820, he later invested it in a grocery and wine and spirits shop in High Street, Kilmarnock, where he blended his own brand of whisky known as *Walker's Kilmarnock Whisky*.

The whisky proved very popular locally while Walker himself, rather ironically, was a teetotaller.

He died in 1857, while his son Alexander Walker and his son George Paterson Walker were responsible for rapidly expanding the whisky business – with Alexander re-naming Walker's Kilmarnock Whisky *Johnnie Walker*.

It was Alexander Walker who, in 1870, was responsible for the introduction of the company's iconic square bottle – which meant more bottles could be fitted into the same space, resulting in fewer breakages while in transit.

An immensely popular international brand, with the blends of White, Red and Black Label, the company joined the Distillers Company in 1925 while Distillers was acquired by Guinness in 1986.

In 1997, Guinness merged with Grand Metropolitan to form Diageo and, in March of 2012, the Johnnie Walker plant – then the largest employer in Kilmarnock – closed its doors after Diageo controversially moved production to its plants in Shieldhall, Glasgow and in Leven, Fife in a major restructuring programme.

Born at Auchinflower, Ayrshire in 1824, Andrew Barclay Walker was a noted nineteenth century brewer and art collector.

Entering his father Peter Walker's brewing business in Ayr and taking control of it following his father's death in 1879, he expanded it into England with the creation of Peter Walker and Son (Warrington and Burton) Ltd.

Serving as Lord Mayor of Liverpool in 1873 and 1876 and as High Sheriff of Lancashire from 1886 to 1877, he was knighted in 1877 and created Baronet Walker of Gateacre, in the County of Lancaster, nine years later.

As an art lover and collector, he built the

Walker Art Gallery, donating it to the City of Liverpool before his death in 1893.

His son William Hall Walker was the politician and Thoroughbred racehorse breeder born in 1856.

As a politician, he served as Conservative MP for Widnes from 1900 until 1919, while as a horse breeder he established a stud farm at Tully, near Kildare town, in Ireland – breeding horses that included the 1906 Epsom Derby winner *Minoru*.

This stud later came to form the basis of what are now the Irish National Stud and the National Stud of the United Kingdom, and now located at Newmarket, Suffolk.

Created Baron Wavertree of Delamere in the County of Chester in 1919, he died in 1953, while in 1999 the *Racing Post* ranked him 24th in its list of Top 100 Makers of 20th Century Horse Racing.

His brother John Reid Walker, born in 1855 and who died in 1934, was a noted polo player and breeder of both polo ponies and racehorses.

One of the famous racehorses he bred, at his Ruckley Stud Farm in Shifnal, Staffordshire was *Invershin*, winner of the Ascot Gold Cup in 1928 and 1929.

From horse racing to golf, George Herbert Walker was the wealthy American businessman and banker who, as a golf enthusiast, served as president of the United States Golf Association (USGA) and in whose honour the USGA's famous biennial golf match the Walker Cup is named.

Born in 1875 in St Louis, Missouri, it was through his daughter Dorothy's marriage to Prescott Bush that he became the maternal grandfather of former American President George H.W. Bush and paternal great-grandfather of former President George W. Bush; he died in 1953.

Chapter four:

On the world stage

Not only a veteran American actress and comedienne of the stage, television and the big screen but also a television and film director, Anna Myrtle Swoyer, better known as Nancy Walker, was born in 1922 in Philadelphia.

Making her Broadway stage debut in 1941 in a production of *Best Foot Forward*, her performance landed her a contract to star beside Lucille Ball in the 1943 film version of the play.

In the same year, she appeared with Judy Garland and Mickey Rooney in *Girl Crazy*, while other film credits include the 1944 *On the Town*.

Nominated for a Tony award in 1956 for her role in the musical revue *Phoenix '55* and also in 1961 for her role, beside Phil Silvers, in *Do Re Mi*, she also recorded versions of show tunes that include *I'm Gonna Wash That Man Right Outa My Hair* and *You Irritate Me So*.

Also known for television roles that include that of Mildred in *McMillan and Wife*, she also directed *The Mary Tyler Moore Show*, appearing in several episodes and also in the show's equally popular spin-off *Rhoda*.

The recipient of an Emmy Award nomination for her role of the widowed sister of the character Sophia Petrillo in *The Golden Girls*, she died in 1992.

Also with a number of television and film credits, **William Walker** was the American actor best known for his role of Reverend Sykes in the 1962 box-office hit *To Kill a Mockingbird*, adapted from the Harper Lee novel of the name.

Born in 1896 in Pendleton, Indiana and with television credits that include *Rawhide*, *The Twilight Zone*, *Daniel Boone* and *Our Man Flint*, in common with Nancy Walker he died in 1992.

Born in 1979 in Montreal, **Andrew W. Walker** is the Canadian actor and producer whose big screen credits include the 2001 *The Score* and the 2006 *Steel Toes*; television credits include *Sabrina, The Teenage Witch*, *ER*, *CSI: Miami* and *The Big Bang Theory*.

Not only an American actor but also the founder of a leading worldwide charity, **Paul William Walker IV** was born in 1973 in Glendale, California.

Best known for his role of Brian O'Connor in the street racing action series of films *The Fast and the Furious* he was, ironically, killed in a car accident in 2013.

Filmed before his death and released posthumously, he also starred in the 2013 *Hours* and the 2014 *Brick Mansions*, while he was the founder of the charity, Reach Out Worldwide (ROWW) that provides humanitarian relief for people living in areas devastated by natural disasters.

Best known for his role of Cheyenne Bodie in the western television series *Cheyenne*, Norman Eugene Walker is the American retired actor, born in 1927 in Hartford, Illinois, better known as **Clint Walker**.

Big screen credits include the 1964 *None But the Brave*, the 1967 *The Dirty Dozen* and, from 1969, *More Dead Than Alive*.

The recipient of a star on the Hollywood Walk of Fame in 2004, he is also an inductee of the Hall of Great Western Performers at the National Cowboy and Western Heritage Museum in Oklahoma City.

Behind the camera lens, **Hal Walker** was the American film director who worked on early Dean Martin and Jerry Lewis films that include the 1950 *At War with the Army* and the 1952 *Sailor Beware*, for which he received an Academy Award nomination.

Born in 1964 in Altoona, Pennsylvania, **Andrew Kevin Walker** is the award-winning American screenwriter who is the recipient of a number of BAFTA nominations for Best Original Screenplay for films that include the 1995 *Seven*, and the 1999 *Sleepy Hollow*.

From film to the world of literature, **Margaret Walker**, née Alexander, was the American poet and writer born in 1915 in Birmingham, Alabama.

Later moving to Chicago and becoming a member of the city's noted African-American literary movement, her award-winning works include her 1942 poem *For My People* and the 1966 American Civil War novel *Jubilee*; she died in 1998.

A noted contemporary African-American writer, **Alice Walker** was born into a poor farming family, the youngest of eight children, in Putnam County, Georgia in 1944.

Best known for her 1982 novel *The Color Purple*, she was aged only eight when she began writing, despite having lost the sight of an eye.

Her best-selling *The Color Purple*, which draws on some of her own experiences as an activist in the 1960s in the civil rights movement, was the winner of a Pulitzer Prize for Fiction and National

Book Award for Fiction in addition to being adapted for the 1985 film of the name and a 2005 Broadway musical.

Other major works include her 1976 *Meridian*, the 1989 *The Temple of My Familiar* and, from 1992, *Possessing the Secret of Joy*.

Bearers of the Walker name have also excelled in the highly competitive world of sport.

On the golf course, **Cyril Walker**, born in Manchester in 1892, was the English professional player who, after immigrating to the United States in 1914, went on to win a series of major titles.

These included the 1916 Indiana Open, the 1924 U.S. Open and six Professional Golfers Association (PGA) events between 1917 and 1930.

Latterly the professional at the Saddle River Golf and Country Club in Paramus, New Jersey he developed an unfortunate relationship with alcohol and ended up working as a dishwasher; near destitute, he died in 1948.

In the high-speed sport of Formula One motor racing, Graeme Murray Walker, better known as **Murray Walker**, is the semi-retired commentator and journalist who for many years was the 'voice' of the sport for the BBC.

Born in 1923 in Hall Green, Birmingham and known for his enthusiastic commentating style, he has also commentated for ITV.

The recipient of an OBE for his contribution to motor racing, his other claim to fame is that while he worked for a time as a copy writer for an advertising agency he coined the slogans "Opal Fruits, made to make your mouth water" and "Trill makes budgies bounce with health."

From sport to music, Noel Scott Engel, born in 1943 in the United States but a UK citizen since 1970, is the singer, songwriter, composer and record producer better known as **Scott Walker**.

As the vocalist for the mid-1960s' band the Walker Brothers, he enjoyed major chart success with hit singles that include *Make it Easy on Yourself*, *My Ship is Coming In* and *The Sun Ain't Gonna Shine Anymore*, while he is also now a successful solo artist.

Born in 1931 in Blytheville, Arkansas, Autry DeWatt Mixon, Jr., was the American musician better known as **Junior Walker**, of the band Junior Walker and the All Stars.

With hits that include the 1965 *Shotgun* and the 1969 *What Does It Take (To Win Your Love)*, he died in 1995.

Ranked by *Rolling Stone* magazine at 67th in its list of The 100 Greatest Guitarists of All Time, Aaron Thibeaux Walker was the American blues guitarist, singer and songwriter better known as **T-Bone Walker**.

Born in 1910 in Linden, Texas and recognised as a pioneer and innovator of electric blues and jump blues and an inductee of the Rock and Roll Hall of Fame, he died in 1975.

Born in 1945 in Napa, California, **Shirley Walker** was the American film and television composer and conductor who has the distinction of having been the first female composer to earn a solo score credit on a major Hollywood film.

This was for her work on the score for the 1992 John Carpenter film *Memoirs of an Invisible Man*, while for television she composed the scores for the 1992 to 1995 series *Batman: The Animated Series* and the 1996 to 2000 *Superman: The Animated Series*.

Winner of a Daytime Emmy Award as music director for *Batman: The Animated Series* and for music composition for the 2001 *Batman Beyond*, she died in 2006.